The Road from West Brom

THE ROAD FROM WEST BROM

GORDON BUNCE

Foreword by Roy Hattersley

SUTTON PUBLISHING

First published in the United Kingdom in 2005 by
Sutton Publishing Limited · Phoenix Mill
Thrupp · Stroud · Gloucestershire · GL5 2BU

British Library Cataloguing in Publication Data
A catalogue record for this book is available from the British Library.

ISBN 0-7509-3988-5

Typeset in 12/17pt ACaslon Regular.
Typesetting and origination by
Sutton Publishing Limited.
Printed and bound in England by
J.H. Haynes & Co. Ltd, Sparkford.

Contents

	Acknowledgements	7
	Foreword by Lord Hattersley	9
	Introduction	11
1	In the Beginning	17
2	A Home for Mice and Men	35
3	Living in Hope	40
4	The Coming of War	59
5	Pleasure & Leisure	67
6	Childhood Memories	80
7	The Death of My Mother	86
8	The Decline of the Black Country and its Industry	90
9	Final Days in West Bromwich	100
10	Welcome to the Grand Hotel	107
11	Through Swing Doors	111
12	It's Too Late Now	126
	About the Author	128

Acknowledgements

While it is not possible to acknowledge all those who have assisted me in the process of putting together this book, there are some to whom I would wish to pay special thanks:

Geoff and Diane Hale
Neill Humphries
Ivor Simpson
Smethwick Reference Library
Solihull Central Library
Black Country Museum, Dudley.

I am indebted to Neil Humphries from Walsall for the photographs which chronicle and bring back to life the working world that once revolved around F. H. Lloyd & Company.

Gordon Bunce

Foreword

It could not happen now. Gordon Bunce spent his childhood in a house so close to the abattoir that he watched the pigs being stunned and slaughtered. His mother died when he was too young to understand death and the next ten years were spent with a loving father and stepmother who, though kind and sympathetic, seem never quite to have filled the gap left so early in his life. Yet a boy from such unpromising beginnings became the director of a great engineering company and a pillar of the industrial Midlands during their postwar heyday.

Gordon Bunce made his journey along a winding route. His father – a chef in the Birmingham Midlands Hotel – expected his son to follow him into the catering trade and, like so many good fathers, hoped that the second generation would enjoy the success which had eluded the first. Young Gordon, immaculate in white tie and tails, waited on Anna Neagle, and so impressed Frank Sinatra that he was asked to join the singer for a drink. Naturally, it was Mrs Sinatra – Ava Gardner – whom Bunce remembered best!

Like many members of his generation, national service changed his life. He fought with the 170 Mortars Royal Artillery in the Korean War of 1950–3 and came back to England with a new perspective on progress and promotion. Then his slow progress through the engineering industry began. Its speed accelerated with the years until he retired from Spear & Jackson, the toolmakers who proudly own a maker's mark from both Sheffield and Wednesbury and between there was some thirty-five years with the Joseph Lucas Electrical Co. Ltd, the then hard grind of qualifications obtained with little help except the drive of personal ambition.

FOREWORD

Had Gordon been born fifty years later, he would have been sent off to a school which offered him the opportunity of examination success and then would have made a seamless transition into university. He might have become an engineer, or he might have read some other subject. And it is possible that between graduation and employment there would have been two or three years with nothing much to do. But he would not, in the phrase of the time, 'have worked his way up'. The experience that makes character and the hard knocks that encourage fortitude would have been denied to him.

Gordon Bunce therefore tells not simply his own story, but the story of a type, a class, a region and a generation. His telling is an autobiography, a chapter of social history. It is essentially the story of a Black Country man.

Nowadays Gordon devotes his spare time to restoring antique toys. When Admiral Nelson went to the Black Country as part of the triumphant tour that followed the Battle of Copenhagen, he mistakenly – and much to the annoyance of the local citizens – called it the 'toy shop of the world'. He should have said the workshop of the world.

It was men like Gordon Bunce who made it so.

Roy Hattersley

Introduction

A Brief History of West Bromwich

The origins of West Bromwich owe much to the southward migration of people such as my ancestors, who probably set out from the north-east region of England, now known as Humberside, in search of greener and more pleasant lands. Here they were to find plentiful supplies of water and land that was both lush and fertile. Wild boar and fowl existed in abundance and the streams and rivers would have been running with freshwater fish.

The most noticeable – or recognisable – feature of the place to these incomers was the sunshine-yellow shrub that proliferated in its meadows, so the area came to be known as the 'place of the broom' or Broomwic. By about 650 a number of settlements had come into existence, so prefixes were added to differentiate one from the other – Little Broomwic, Castle Broomwic and our own West Broomwic.

Like those in other parts of the realm, the original pastoral settlers were troubled on a fairly regular basis by invaders and usurpers. As each wave passed on or retreated, some of its people remained to become part of the landscape. One of the Saxon lords who passed this way, Wulfhere, went on to lord it over a piece of high ground we now know as Wolverhampton, although it may be that its name has more to do with another Saxon, Lady Wulfrun, who granted substantial lands to the Church in 985 and is commemorated in a statue in the city.

Wednesbury had attained borough status as early as 916 and around the same time Birmingham had its beginnings as the settlement of Berm's people. Smithwick was established, as its name indicates, on heathland, Lichfield in a watery and marshy area, and another farming community was created by a chief called Hondes at Handsworth.

Despite unwelcome attention from the Danes in around 800 – Wednesbury was the furthest point of their incursions into the British Isles –

This 'atmospheric' image of North Staffordshire in the 1930s gives an idea of the setting of our daily lives with the outpourings of the factories clouding and blackening the landscape.

Taken on a summer's day in the early 1930s, this photograph shows how the Black Country got its name. The pollution is so thick that even the sun is not visible.

West Bromwich and its neighbours began to settle down to peace and prosperity, at least until the arrival of the Normans, but even by 1380 it only numbered about 160 souls among its population.

In 1743 when John Wesley came to Wednesbury the citizens of that place were as pleased to see him as they had been the Danes and he had to be rescued from the hands of a self-righteous mob. West Bromwich too has had its share of riotous behaviour, notably on the accession of the Hanoverians when insurgents from Wolverhampton and Sedgley swelled the local throng and battle with the authorities was enjoined at six in the evening of 12 July 1715. I need not report that King George and his forces got the better of the debate and the objectors were dealt with in the manner of the time (without counselling).

Although nail and gun making had gone on for many years in a small way, West Bromwich's was a rural economy until the latter years of the eighteenth century. The building of a canal through Gold's Green in 1769 was the initial catalyst for change which, when it came, was both rapid and total. A coal mine was established at Wednesbury, scarring and redefining the landscape and bringing with it a new kind of invasion – of skilled miners, of entrepreneurs and of migrant labour. At the same time those with the wherewithal moved away from the ugly source of industrial wealth to dwell in more salubrious regions such as Tipton and Hill Top. The coal was desperately needed to fuel the burgeoning iron industry and West Bromwich, its agricultural past disappearing under a blackening cloud of dust, the place of the yellow shrubs, yielded to a new broom and a future inexorably linked to Britain's industrial destiny.

All things must pass. In 1750, almost 600 years after it was built, Dudley Castle was destroyed by fire with the locals looking on paralysed by the thought that it contained gunpowder. Alterations to Carter's Green in 1835 turned up the body of a Mr Edward Lane interred there a mere sixty years previously with a stake driven through his body to deter fellow would-be suicides.

Now the area's industrial star has waned and it adjusts itself for whatever fate awaits it; whatever role it is up for in the new millennium. Even its distinctive 'Black Country' vernacular is a-gooin' the way of all flesh. When I lived there in the 1930s a pall hung over the place. Its canals were dirty and polluted, with household rubbish and even with the bodies of cats and dogs. The water was oily and there was no notion of these once great feats of engineering as scenic attractions for visitors, merely as a convenient receptacle for waste and, more than once, a handy solution for those whose lives were so utterly miserable that the prospect of posthumous staking seemed little reason not to emulate the aforementioned Mr Lane. Violence of one kind and another was endemic at all levels of society. There were brawls every Saturday night and wife-beating was an accepted hazard. On the other hand, kids played outside until all hours, in safety for the most part, and vandalism was unheard of.

This then was my birthplace and I cannot say that during my time there things got much better. In fact, in many ways they went from bad to worse as the place lost its way as an industrial centre and went into decline. But there was a spirit of the place and of the people that makes me still proud to call West Bromwich, the Black Country and Staffordshire – the county to which, at heart, regardless of foolish political tinkerings, it still belongs – my home and the place from which I come.

1

In the Beginning

I was born Gordon Thomas Bunce on Friday 9 September 1932 at the Alum Hospital, West Bromwich, Staffordshire (now Sandwell, West Midlands). The Thomas bit came from my grandfather. I have to believe that my birth was a blessing and a happy event, though new babies were by no means a rarity in those days. All around were families who were clearly ill-equipped to support one child yet whose progeny seemed to multiply every year. Everywhere you

Hallam Hospital had only been in existence for five years when I was born there on 9 September 1930. This photograph shows it in its original incarnation, as the infirmary and poorhouse in 1884. The whole has now been absorbed into Sandwell Hospital.

Grandfather Thomas Wallace poses in his Sunday best at Union Street in 1935. He said little and grunted a lot.

looked poor mothers trudged behind prams containing one or more infants while others of varying ages shuffled alongside until they reached the magical age of five and the law demanded their presence at one of the newly provided state schools.

The 1930s were a difficult period all round and nowhere more so than in the Black Country. Whole families could be out of work for long periods and we were fortunate that my father at least found something from time to time, though it must have been poorly paid judging by our standard of living as seen from this distance. Of course, back then I knew no different and assumed this was the norm for everyone at all times.

The Black Country got its name from the coal and iron ore deposits found between Wolverhampton in the north and Birmingham in the south. The South Staffordshire coalfield covered Bloxwich, Wednesbury and Tipton and extended as far as Dudley, creating what was essentially a huge basin of the two highly sought after minerals. The discovery of these resources in the course of the nineteenth century turned a big piece of merry England into a nightmarish industrial landscape with crimson skies and sulphurous fumes. A layer of grime covered everything and many went to an early grave, their lungs caked with the fallout from the countless chimney stacks that belched without ceasing, and the dust from the slag heaps that were an equal blight upon the land and everything that lived upon it. No one would choose to live in such a place; those who did had exhausted any other choices. Their accommodation was squalid at best; more often than not the properties they were forced to rent had been condemned as dangerous, with subsiding foundations and structural faults. No residents' associations protected them; there was no legal recourse. Their landlords told them to pay their few shillings rent and be

This idealised image of the Earl of Dudley's coal pits contains all the elements I remember of the Black Country – coal, smoke, dirt and factories – but depicted more in the way his lordship would have liked them to be remembered than as they were in reality.

A postcard from West Bromwich with some general views of the town.

thankful. Compared to the alternatives of which they were all too aware, most were just that.

Of course, not everyone in England was subject to quite such privations and in retrospect it's tempting to wonder why more people didn't move away. Travel was neither easy nor part of most people's experience before the Second World War. And there was no guarantee that grass would be greener – some two-thirds of the British population lived in slum conditions and suffered from malnutrition.

It is fair to say then that most of the men in employment in West Bromwich in those times had something to do with the mines or the steel producing mills – iron smelters, colliers, pitmen, furnace workers and those on the surface or outside the factory gates that fed the industrial machine or transported its products beyond the region. Coarse and ill-educated, most were kindly people who would do what they could to help others from the little they themselves had.

It's all as clear in my mind as if it were yesterday. My earliest recollections are of my grandparents' home in Union Street, off Spon Lane. They lived in one of a number of one up, one down houses fronting on an open earth courtyard. The houses were approached through an entry or alley, which became a 6ft wide footpath of blue brick. This was very uneven with many bricks missing and others sinking into the mud. I remember that you had to walk with great diligence to avoid catching your feet. Sprained ankles were commonplace.

On one side of the courtyard was the communal brewhouse or wash house. This, as the latter name suggests, was where all the residents did their weekly wash. Its other title came from the fact that in years gone by real ale had been brewed in the same copper bowls that now served for laundry. On the other side was another communal facility, often in greater demand, the loo.

Little now remains of Union Street, but on the wall of the Cricketer's Arms you can still make out the outline of the pigeon loft that stood against it in the old yard.

My grandmother and grandfather in the yard at Union Street, 1930s.

In the arms of my grandfather, Thomas Wallace, as a two-month-old baby.

A communal washhouse or brewhouse existed in the yards of many of the old back-to-back houses, though most had only one coal-fired tub. The one pictured above was probably commercially operated.

Responsibilities for these communal facilities were shared by all the families who lived in the yard. Both were dank and smelly summer and winter, but the loo was often indescribable, the persistently vile smell and the attentions of the thousands of flies attracted by it making visits hellish. There was no proper plumbing, simply an earth thunderbox – a wooden box with a hole cut in it – for a seat. The door was constructed from a few old planks nailed together as a nod to privacy, but the number and variety of holes in the planks rendered the exercise largely ineffective, leaving occupants feeling very exposed.

A curious feature of my granddad's house was his wireless. Bearing in mind that radio broadcasting didn't begin until 1928, it seems incongruous to say the least that he should have possessed such an elaborate and costly thing in the early '30s. It consisted of a black box with two large dials on it – one,

The remains of the old Methodist school in Union Street, now used as warehousing. The small chapel on the right is where I was baptised.

I imagine, was the volume control, the other the tuner. The sound emerged from a huge copper speaker in the shape of a horn. I have always believed my granddad to be an honest man – indeed he must have had a legitimate explanation for its acquisition, or it would not have been on open display, dominating as it did the small living room.

The wireless left little space for the scrubbed table and grime-blackened chairs. Next to the window which overlooked the yard was a deep glazed earthenware sink. Any lighting in the cramped and dingy room was supplied by gas. I believe there was also a black cast-iron stove, but my recollections of this are hazy. It would have been normal to do all the cooking on the range in those days. This stood against one of the walls and, as a matter of pride, was kept blackened and polished by my grandmother with her trusty 'Zebro'. The house had a perpetual smell of carbolic and castor oil and there would always be water boiling on the hob in a huge and equally black kettle. I don't know

This was taken between the wars and shows a dwelling very similar to my grandparents' house, where I first lived. This woman doesn't even have a brewhouse, so has to do her washing outside in all weathers.

whether some other form of heating and storing hot water existed – a kettle no matter how large seems very inadequate to supply grandfather's bath when he came home from work encrusted in grime. In so small a room modesty was a luxury and privacy in very short supply. I can't recall that it troubled me as a small boy, but have often wondered how the family felt when my grandfather bared all and stood in the tin bath while my grandmother scrubbed him down. I recall that his body was surprisingly white in sharp contrast to his arms and his head which were a deep, almost black, red in colour.

Grandad worked at the Kendrick steel mill in Union Street. At around the age of 5 I was often given the task of taking food to him at work. Usually some kind of stew, this was prepared by my grandmother in a pudding basin tied with a coloured cloth to keep it warm. I well remember taking the basin and its contents to the steelworks, walking in through the entrance and experiencing the momentary blindness before my eyes became accustomed to

An old fire grate or range similar to the one we had before the war at Union Street.

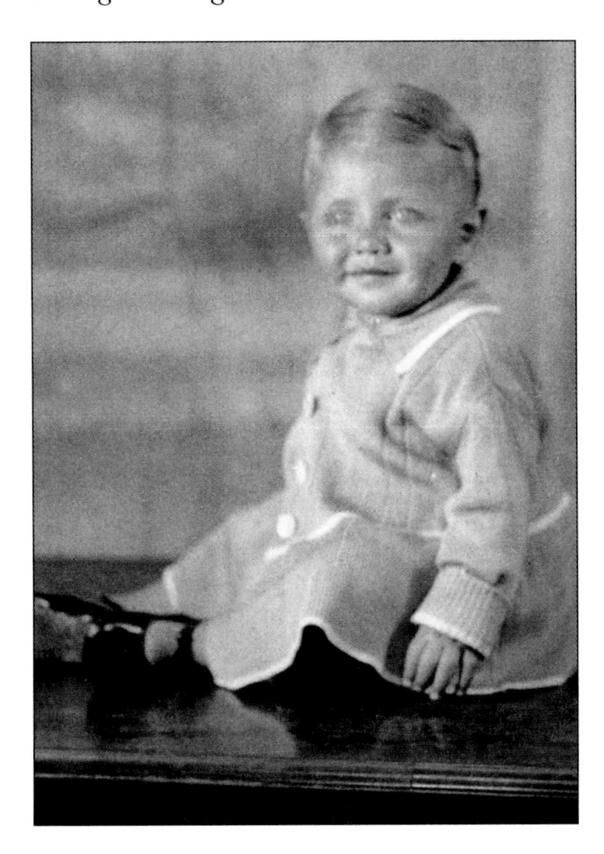

Here I am perched on a table at 12 months old. Hopefully somebody was standing by to catch me.

the blackness within. Then I would move along the inside of the foundry past the seething furnaces. Huge lashes of molten metal would throw out from these without warning, striking terror into my young heart, but fortunately I never came to any harm. The interior of the foundry was always so dark that the white hot metal was all the more dazzling when it emerged into the sulphurous atmosphere and seared through the cloud that forever hung just above ground level. The river of molten steel ran through channels into the waiting moulds. Then, using large pincers that hung from the overhead gantries on wires, one of the workers would transfer the moulds to another part of the foundry.

A by-product of the steel works was iron cast billets that resembled giant machines. These were dumped on an adjacent waste area and, with their climbing possibilities and the holes that had been drilled in their metal frames

A portrait of a typical Black Country working man. Even in front of the photographer in his 'Sunday best', he couldn't be without his Woodbine or his flat cap.

– often large enough for a child to crawl through – made the perfect place to play for a while after discharging the meal delivery duties. I don't recall anyone ever being told to play somewhere else, or warned of the dangers of being injured or trapped by the casts. Neither do I remember anyone being trapped or badly injured. Perhaps a stronger instinct for survival was able to exist in the complete absence of today's mollycoddling and restrictive regulations.

Despite their hard times and being worn out well before their time, our grandparents always had time for us, and miraculously would always find a copper for some sweets from the corner shop. My grandmother died in 1939 having barely reached her fifty-ninth birthday, suffering from heart trouble and so bloated that the folds of her swollen ankles hung over her feet and shoes.

It's difficult to imagine now how we all managed to crowd into my grandparents' tiny house for as long as we did, and it must have been a great relief when my parents could move out to their own home in Friar Park. This was a kind of overspill area of West Bromwich built near the boundary with Wednesbury in around 1930, one of a number of schemes to move people from the squalor of the town's back-to-back houses partly to provide an opportunity for their demolition. With hindsight we were especially fortunate to move when we did, as the advent of the Second World War put many of these already overdue plans on hold and it would be the 1950s before moves to rid West Bromwich of its slum dwellings would again be put in train.

At that time I was unaware of the existence of the tool works known as Elwell's Forge, although it was situated near our new Friar Park home, in Coronation Road. This forge, just over the boundary in Wednesbury, would eventually become the famous Spear & Jackson tool company – and I would be its director – but that was still far in the future. The Elwell Forge, and indeed the Elwell family, were well known and highly respected throughout the Black Country, being then especially generous benefactors to the town of Wednesbury, but neither left any lasting impression on my childhood world. I can visualise the canal that ran past our new house in Carisbrooke Road, and the times I would run down to the towpath to watch the barges on their way to mysterious destinations in the wider world. From this distance they seemed like sullen people with no waves or smiles to return. No doubt their waterborne existence seemed less romantic from their viewpoint, the business of transporting the coal as much a daily grind as winning it from the mines – and probably no more financially rewarding. I waved and smiled all the same from my canalside playground. I would be aghast these days at the thought of an infant playing unsupervised on a canal towpath. Back then it surprised or alarmed no one.

My aunt and uncle lived close to us in Carisbrooke Road, and I tend to remember their house more than my own. It was closer to the canal near to where it was crossed by a footbridge. The only other strong recollection I have

Opposite: My mother, Gladys Bunce (née Wallace). Her life seemed like a catalogue of suffering and hardship. I hope she experienced some joy along the way. After seeing her go through so much it did seem to the family that her death was a blessed release.

Right: A view along the Tame Valley canal with the local council houses visible at the top of the bank on the left. Our house was by the bridge seen in the distance.

from the period at Friar Park is of the funfair that was held nearby with its annual ox-roast.

Soon, however, we were on the move again – I suspect because the rent had become too much for Father. For ordinary people, property or accommodation hunting – like that for employment – had then to be done on foot. My mother trooped from estate agent to letting agent, and then trudged all over the place to view the accommodations. Most once reached were slum dwellings well past their demolition date – many would need no demolition as they were falling down of their own accord. In one house the paper was curling off the walls from the running damp and the floor was six inches from the skirting board – a direct result of the mines criss-crossing the earth beneath, into which it and many of its kind were slowly subsiding. Worn out and disillusioned, my mother related her lack of success to my father on his return from work. Fortunately, soon after he was able to find us a house in Edward Street, close to Carter's Green and the Accident Hospital. During our time there I was the hospital's star patient, forever being patched up after one accident or another. My father was in what was known as a 'Saturday fund', so the cost of treatment was taken care of. When I think now of the number of times I had to be taken to that hospital, the fund must have been completely exhausted.

Many of the houses near Edward Street were derelict and falling down, providing an irresistible playground for a young lad, full of curiosity and looking for opportunities for mischief. Getting into trouble came naturally to

A view along Edward Street. Our house was about five in from the far end on the left-hand side. The abattoir was right at the end, in more ways than one.

Dad, George, at 26 when his ambitions and hopes were still intact. Sadly, in one way or another they would be frustrated in later life.

me and at times it must have proved a real burden to my mother in particular who, unknown to me, already had her fair share of problems.

In our garden when we arrived was the body of a Morgan sports car. There wasn't much left of it and it had apparently been housed in a tumbledown shed or garage, but it was more than enough to fire my imagination and create a world in which I was a famous racing driver. What was then an abandoned and seemingly worthless plaything would probably be highly valued today.

Another aspect of life very different to the present was the local abattoir, sited near our dwellings, into which I could wander as a child. I watched the animals being driven up a ramp to where a man with a gun would despatch them. From there they would fall into the inner part of the building where I presume they were butchered and prepared for the meat markets.

We moved so many times in my life that I sometimes think the name of Bunce should apply to a nomadic tribe. I had been happy in the house in Edward Street and was sorry that we were once more on our way. Nobody told me why, but all other things apparently being equal, it is safe to assume shortage of money was at the bottom of it. As the saying goes, 'What's new?'

Any such shortage of funds was not brought about by drinking or gambling. Throughout his life my father was a moderate drinker, and I never knew him waste any money on the horses. His only vice was his Woodbine cigarettes. Sometimes on a Saturday lunchtime, he would take me to the pub, where I would play outside with the other children, eating crisps and drinking pop. He was also a great fan of the cinema. He loved to scan the papers and choose a film we could all go and see – mostly, as I recall, cowboys or war films. I don't think these were the films my mother would have chosen, and she didn't always come along with us. Happy times, nonetheless.

But now we were on the move again. Such belongings as we had were packed on a handcart – there was little to contend with in the way of furniture, so the handcart and my father's legs were sufficient for the removal process.

Another home, another set of memories were now behind us and we prepared ourselves for the next chapter as we followed the handcart to Hope Street.

2

A Home for Mice and Men

Hope Street was conveniently placed between the New Birmingham Road and Beeches Road, the first of which led to the town centre, the second to Dartmouth Park. Even by today's standards number 43 was a large house; sadly not a good one, but it was a roof and it became a home. I believe it had been built in the late nineteenth century, so the fact that it was still standing had to be a point in its favour. It had been one of those Victorian town houses beloved of the more well-to-do at the turn of the century, but they had long since moved on. There was no front garden; just a wall, behind which a few slabs ran to the front door and the coal cellar grating. The front door was green and I have a feeling the reason this has stayed so vivid in my memory is that in the '30s nearly all front doors were green. Brown and black were the only alternatives I can remember seeing.

The green front door opened on to a hallway from which three doors led off. The first to the front room, the furthest to the sitting room and a centre door that led to the cellar. At the far end of the passage was a glass covered area – veranda or conservatory – with a further three doors: one to the garden, one to the other end of the sitting-room and the third to the backroom. This last was very dimly lit and contained a small leaded grate with a small oven. It had also two chairs and a table, which left barely a chair's width between their occupants and the fire. A home made rug completed the inventory of the tiny room which was otherwise devoid of any home comforts.

An open way led from this room to the so-called kitchen and washhouse. This contained a big copper boiler heated by a small range, but did not really qualify as a kitchen since all cooking was done on the leaded grate in the little room. Beyond the washhouse a further door led you outside to the loo – as before, an earth closet with a wooden plank seat. A garden with two trees completed the picture, though I swear in all the years we lived there I never saw anyone tend it.

Number 43 needed to be big. As well as my own family, it had to accommodate my uncle and aunt and eventually their daughter, Christine. It should be pointed out that my uncle also kept a completely mad dog chained up in a kennel in the garden, but more of this later.

Bagnall Street was typical of those that connected the Birmingham New Road to Beeches Road. It was named after the Bagnall family who were leading ironfounders at Gold's Hill.

Whatever presence the house might once have possessed was already a distant memory. When we moved in it was in full decline and well past its sell-by date. There was no furniture in the front room, and a three-piece suite in 'leather-style' and matching mildew occupied the otherwise bare middle room. This was not made the cosier by the fact that there was never a fire lit in the house other than in the leaded grate and wash boiler. To say it was a cold house would be a masterpiece of understatement. In the winter months the chill reached your very bones.

The upstairs housed three bedrooms and a further set of stairs leading to the attic. Everything was damp and dank. Everyone seemed to accept this as normal and we grew up with the same attitude, never questioning why or whether others might be better off. Perhaps no one was, and all lived with the permanent chill.

Thankfully, the love of my father and mother made up for the lack of warmth in the house. But even at my tender years I sensed the problems and despair of people who, through no fault of their own, were doomed to a life of endless drudgery. Mother was often poorly, prone to rheumatic heart problems that made her rather frail. Father was strong and fit but a man worn out before his years. In the '30s there was little support for those out of work. Such meagre financial support as the government offered came only after subjection to the despised 'means test'. Many people in the Black Country lived on the so-called 'bread line'. Those in work could be said to be comfortable, though not in the sense that we would define the word today. There were no motor cars or luxury goods. One or two, I recall, ran motorcycle and sidecar combinations, but most could barely afford bus fare and would rise early enough to walk to work.

The other most memorable feature about the house in Hope Street was its colony of mice. They infested every nook and cranny of the place and would play together in open defiance of the house's rightful owners. We had no cat, but it's doubtful if one would have made much difference. The property's overall mouldiness and dirty corners provided a perfect mousey dwelling.

This is the main road from Birmingham as it enters West Bromwich. Today it is crossed by the M5 motorway. Hope Street is on the left, just out of the picture.

If number 43 had been a council house, maybe it would have been scrubbed and fumigated. Private individuals had neither the will nor the money for such operations. They just got on with it and tried not to draw the problem to anyone's attention.

My father mainly kept going with labouring jobs. Whatever he did had two things in common, long hours and low pay. Taking his best suit to the pawnbroker's on Monday and taking it out for him on Friday became part of my normal weekly routine. When I discussed the way we lived with other people later in my life, it became clear that they were concerned about the social stigma of being so poor. This was more real to them than the dreadful fact of life as it was lived in those days by the majority of people in this country. Sympathetic as they were, their 'oh dears' did not really take account of the fact that you were too busy just surviving to worry about your social status or any stigma that might apply.

I never felt any reason for shame. Given a level playing field, my family would have been as materially successful as any other. As it was, we were poor. It was simply part of my life in the 1930s, as it was for countless others in the same time and place.

But if we are to achieve a clear understanding of the life of West Bromwich and its people in those far off days, we must go back as nearly as we can manage to the beginning of things. I can't claim that our family was anything particular or 'special'. Probably this exercise would be less interesting to others if we were. Uniqueness and individuality were not looked for in those times. Most people were cut from the same cloth, had the same concerns and shared the same limited goals.

Viewed now, black and white images have a quaintness and simplicity that make their times seem slower, more personal, less demanding. We must remind ourselves that the opposite is the case. The demands of survival were more urgent, the rat-race to secure employment and food more frantic, and the worth of the individual more lowly than we in these easy times can begin to imagine.

3

Living in Hope

Now we've set the stage with a description of the house in Hope Street and its particular foibles, we can begin to bring it to life again by peopling it with the personalities who lived their lives there.

We moved into the house somewhere around June 1938, our possessions transported there by means of a handcart. Where my father would have come by such a thing, I don't know. Perhaps it was borrowed from someone on the market in the town. As well as Father, Mother and myself, the house was to accommodate my uncle, George Wallace, his wife Evelyn and, later, their baby, Christine. After the death of my grandmother, Grandfather would also come to stay. So, large though it was, it was a somewhat crowded house.

As I was by then of school age, it was necessary for my mother to deliver me to the infant and junior school in Beeches Road. I still have a clear image of what seemed to me at 5 like a giant rocking horse, The school was very acceptable to me from day one! I was sorry to discover on revisiting the school recently that all trace of the horse is now gone.

At the end of the school day my mother would come to collect me and would often take me across the road to the wonderland of Dartmouth Park, but this didn't go on for long. Since the school was at one end of Beeches Road and we lived at the other, it was considered safe enough for me to find my own way home. There was hardly any traffic anyway, so I was in little

Beeches Road Junior & Infant School for boys and girls was opened in 1893. Following its centenary, it was renamed after King George V.
A dozen and more years later it became a listed building and its magnificent clock tower was restored to its original bright colours – something that would have been wasted on it when the area was at the peak of its industrial era.

Beeches Road has been much carved up over the years, but the school can be seen in its new found isolation from the West Bromwich bypass.

physical danger. A far more present danger was that, in the absence of parental guidance, I might just wander off into the park, which I did on many an occasion, losing all track of time and returning wide-eyed to my frantic mother hours later than expected. Thankfully I never fell prey to any undesirable types. They seemed less present than they do today, but that is not to say they didn't exist.

A memory that often comes back to me is of fetching Granddad's ale from the pub at the bottom of the street. I'd take his empty bottle to the off-sales counter (or jug 'n' bottle). They would draw the ale from a barrel into a measuring jug, then pour it into the bottle with the aid of a brass funnel.

The infant class I was to attend in the 1930s. It is now a junior class and the vestibule to the left of the picture has now evolved into a handy cubby hole and storage area.

The boys are distinctly outnumbered in this rather posed looking photograph of a nature study class in 1905. In fact there's only one to be seen – poor lad.

The law required that beer served to minors must be in a sealed bottle, so they would put a paper seal over the stopper before pushing it back into the neck of the bottle. If you had the inclination (or the strength) to take out the stopper and taste the contents, the disturbance to the seal would give you away. That was the theory anyway.

Another regular errand was to carry Granddad's accumulator (or battery) down to the ironmongers for recharging. Nothing must be allowed to interrupt the outpourings of his prized radio, so a spare accumulator was kept at the ironmongers fully charged and 'ever ready'. If all the families had radios, the ironmonger must have had a lot of floorspace given over to battery charging.

A class photograph taken in the 1920s. Note the variation in dress.

The modern classroom is more colourful and welcoming, but the principles are not that far removed and the children's work is displayed on the same walls that played host to their parents' and grandparents'.

One of the greatest things about life in Hope Street was being taken by my uncle to see 'the Baggies' – West Bromwich Albion – play at the Hawthorns. This was an even better treat than giving me threepence, or even sixpence, as he sometimes did. I was very fond of my uncle and he was kind to me. He was called up on the outbreak of the Second World War and sustained injuries to his leg from which he would never recover. When, still later, they wanted to remove his leg, he refused and continued to be crippled by it until he died. The only thing I didn't like about him was the mad dog he kept chained in our back garden. The wild mongrel should never have been allowed to live on this earth. It was only let loose when he was alone with it and we were all safely shut in the house.

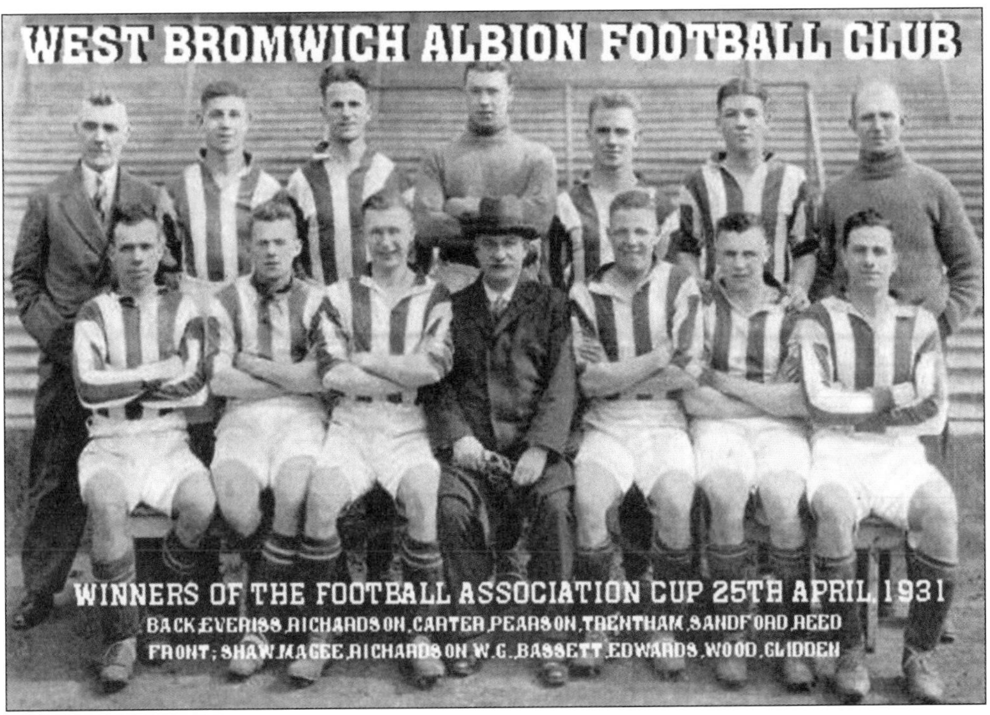

A photograph of the triumphant Albion team that beat Birmingham City 2–1 to win the FA Cup in the 1930/31 season. It was also at this time that they gained promotion to the second division. W.G. Richardson (second from the left, front row) was the hero of the day ('man of the match' as we would now say), having scored the winning goal against Charlton that secured promotion and both goals in the final at Wembley.

Unfortunately, on one occasion it got loose of its own accord and attacked me. It was pulled off me, but not before it had damaged me in several places. On another occasion it bit the end off my friend Peter's finger. His dad was a policeman and insisted that the dog was put down, but it wasn't – not until it got loose again and managed to get into the garden of a house where they bred alsations. It killed one and injured another two so badly they had to be put down. I think then it was either shot or put down later. Either way, to my great relief, it never returned to trouble us in Hope Street.

Occasionally Father would take us out to a sports club on Beeches Road where you could watch a cricket match in the afternoon and stay for a sort of concert in the evening. The show mostly consisted of singers, with a comedian thrown in for good measure. I can remember people laughing but we kids found it deadly boring and usually excused ourselves and hung around outside with a bottle of pop until the grown ups had had their fill and it was time to go home.

A lot of life was lived outside in those days and it really does seem that the weather then was as it should be. Summers were warm and sunny and people would sit out on their front doorsteps just enjoying it as a family. Some people even brought chairs out and spilled into the street, creating a magical communal atmosphere.

In many ways having no spare money made life simpler. Our 'entertainment' was free, or very close to it. Our entire life was centred around things that didn't cost money. Within these obvious limits we were still turned out well. My mother scrubbed me until I shined and on special occasions would apply a blob of margarine before hair combing for that special glossy look. Plain tap water was the everyday hair preparation.

Other families in the street included the Stewarts (just up the road from us), the Butlers (opposite) and (down the road) the Coopers. Mr Cooper was a bus inspector, which was then a very important position. It was considered to be on a par with being a policeman at a time when the law retained its majesty and the public's highest respect. The Coopers had a daughter somewhat older than myself. I wonder where she and the other kids are now, what lives they managed to forge for themselves, and whether they like me are reminiscing about those times now they have children, even grandchildren of their own.

At the top of Hope Street was the Vicarage, where the vicar's major earthly mission was keeping us out of his apple orchard. Many was the time he caught me there, issuing stern warnings of dire consequences should I repeat my trespasses against him, but neither the threatened wrath nor any revelation of wrongdoing came upon me until I reflected in adulthood what a sore trial we must have been. The miracle of 'Adam's garden' was not to be. Cast out for the final time these many years since, the guilt has caught up with us and I can now understand the concept that he didn't grow them for our benefit!

Dartmouth Park was a kids' delight. It was well kept and, in the summer, would draw hundreds of families for days out and picnics. The boating pool was the place to be and, if you were lucky, you could persuade some older lad to take you out.

Above and overleaf: These old and sad gates once formed part of the majestic looking entrance to Dartmouth Park. In its glory days they led to a drive of wonderfully laid out flower borders. Alas, now they form an entrance no more, having been cut off by the West Bromwich bypass. The sweet shop opposite is also long gone. All that remains is a patch of open ground.

The bandstand in happier times recalls the park as it still lives in my memory, when it was our own private wonderland, just along the road from Beeches Road School.

Beyond the park was the area known as Woosan. In those days this large open area was out of bounds as it was known not to be safe. Much of it was undermined and there were unprotected and unmarked open ventilation shafts camouflaged by the undergrowth. Today the area has been made safe and gives pleasure to thousands of people as a sports and leisure facility, providing boating, sailing, golf and excellent walking trails.

My mother would sometimes take me with her on shopping trips to West Bromwich High Street, which then featured most of the well-known shops of the time – Mason's, the Co-op, Woolworth's and Maypole – as well as the indoor market and more local traders, but it was probably not something she relished. Like most young children I wanted everything I saw and had no idea of the value or scarcity of money. I'm sure I gave her a hard time in more ways than one, though I like to think no more than most headstrong young lads would have done.

On one occasion, for no earthly reason I am now able to divine, I simply wandered off, travelling by bus to Great Bridge, which in those days before the advent of the private car was some distance away. I visited an old lady relation of my aunt's; someone with whom I was not at all well acquainted. I could not have been more than 6 years old. For her part, she was probably glad of a visitor of any sort, so she gave me something to eat and let me stay there all day. Back in Hope Street I had become a 'missing person' and unbeknown to me a great hue and cry was going on. How the message got back about where I was I don't know, but eventually my father just came and took me home.

As its name suggests, Dartmouth Park once formed part of the estate of the Dartmouth family. Little trace of their grand house now remained but for a gateway which in my time was a favourite haunt, providing a haven for us kids to play in. It became all the more so on the outbreak of war when the area beyond it was used as a training and testing ground for tanks. We lads loved to watch them lumbering across what had once been fields, churning up the undergrowth and scattering all before them.

My mother's illness became progressively worse and it was felt that some country air would provide a respite from the impoverished atmosphere of West Bromwich. Her sister, Violet, lived with her own family in Upminster Bridge in rural Essex. There was a small wood and a stream near the house in Bennett's Road and my cousin John and I would devise great games with these as a perfect backdrop. In those days Bennett's Road had to be entered by way of an 'unadopted' track that was so potholed traders would refuse to go down it, for fear of breaking the axles on their carts.

Although these visits were made with the main intention of improving my mother's health, they also served as the nearest thing we would know to a holiday. We would make excursions to Grays and Southend, visiting the famous Kursaal funfair and paddling in the sea. Since my uncle was an

Above: The imposing, if not positively intimidating, Sandwell Lodge entrance arch.

Right: The Sandwell Arch a few years ago, decaying and neglected. Once the proud entrance to the estate of the second Baron of Dartmouth, it had already ceased to fulfil that function long before the time when I used to play there as a kid. The 'murkiness of the Black Country skies' was, it seems, not to baronial tastes and the Dartmouth family removed themselves to somewhere with a cleaner atmosphere. I remember the arch well, and the small gate alongside which gave access to the clubhouse of the Sandwell Park golf club. During the war years the grounds and the area towards Handsworth cemetery were used for tank exercises. Eventually the arch found itself abandoned on a roundabout amid the link roads for the West Bromwich bypass and the M5, but I'm happy to report that extensive renovations have been put in hand to protect it and restore some of its former glory. I don't think it will see service as a playground for small boys again in the foreseeable future.

engineer on the railway at Upminster, travel was practically free. The electric trains finished at Upminster, then steam trains took over from there to the coast. These were idyllic times for me. Essex was wonderful – even more so when contrasted with life in West Bromwich. My aunt and uncle's house was on the edge of a cornfield in a small village. There was a little farm at the top of the road where you could get eggs and such. Life was totally different and inevitably I began to be envious of the people who lived in that warm, soft-focus landscape.

By contrast, back home people were living in a grey world, men in their patched-to-death trousers and jackets – my own shorts and handed down clothes no exception. Most lads would have their heads shaved, except for a tufted bit at the front. This was not so much a fashion as a precaution against head lice, which were nonetheless commonplace. In fact fleas and lice were so much a part of life that their presence was not considered sufficient reason to send a child home from school.

Sadly, brief sojourns in the country were not enough to reverse my mother's decline. When she eventually died that dreamworld died with her; its warmth and its hope succumbed to the grey grime that blanketed everything else and real life ground on.

* * *

My father gave me sixpence pocket money, which was enough to buy a bag of 'speck' (not quite rotten) fruit, get you into the Saturday morning cinema and buy you a drink of cordial. If you caught the bus to town you had to do without the cordial, that is unless you could duck the conductor and get away without paying. The town was only a few stops away, so we would head for the opposite part of the bus to the conductor. If he was upstairs, we would go down, and vice versa. With any luck he wouldn't reappear before our stop. Either way, we would rush for the exit knowing he would only be able to stop one or two of us. If anyone was caught for the ticket price, we would share our cordial with them in the cinema.

Charlie Collett behind the counter of the Period Shop. This amazing shop is a reconstruction of the kind of general provisioners we had back in the 1930s. If you had gas lighting you could buy a new mantle here, if you had oil lamps you came here for your paraffin. You could leave your accumulator for recharging and purchase almost anything imaginable. The shop still stands, having been built in 1895.

I'm always coaxing Charlie to dress up in this genuine Black Country attire, so he will blend in with the shop's atmosphere.

Most cinemas were little better than flea pits, but the Tower in Carter's Green was an exception. Films were so valuable in those days as a release from reality – somewhere to escape to. Their actors had real 'star' status; everybody knew them and what kind of film they would be in. Gene Autry was the great cowboy star and I particularly loved the comedy films of Stan Laurel and Oliver Hardy. Tarzan was a huge hit with the boys, and there was also home-grown comedy from the likes of Old Mother Riley and her daughter Kitty.

A surprising number of the films we watched then have stood the test of time. Others, of course, have become dated. This has caused them to be dismissed as in some way worthless. Many of today's films will also become dated, but that does not devalue them. Their value in their own time was immeasurable and the key they hold to the attitudes and tastes of those times should never be undervalued.

Nowadays the cinema doesn't attract people in such numbers. To take a family to a movie can cost more than twenty pounds, in return for which you get that one film and endless adverts and trailers. For ninepence we got a 'full supporting feature' with a cartoon and a newsreel in addition to the 'main feature'. Posh types paid a shilling and went upstairs.

The Clock Tower at Carter's Green from which the Tower cinema, which stood opposite (to the left of this picture), got its name. The Tower opened on Monday 9 December 1935. Its first feature film was Hitchcock's *The Thirty-Nine Steps* starring Robert Donat and local West Bromwich girl Madeleine Carroll. The building was demolished some years ago.

Such were the times. They could be like a living hell for some folk. People scrimped for everything they had in a society that had become used to living from hand to mouth. There was no option to drop out and take handouts from a government department. Pay was low even for those who were working, but for many, particularly older people, life must have been very difficult indeed. The term 'them and us' was no joke in those days. Members of the upper-class could spend more on a cigar than a working man earned in a day. Nowadays ever more people are living from plastic – supporting their lifestyle with credit card debt. Back then the pawnbroker was how you extended your wages. When that avenue was closed you turned to friends and relations if you had any. If not, your luck ran out.

4

The Coming of War

It sounds like a terrible thing to say that the Second World War was the best thing that ever happened to the people of the Black Country, but the old cliché about an ill wind holds true. Most people talk about the privations and shortages the war caused in their daily lives, but you needed to have had those things in the first place in order to miss them. When you start with nothing, there's nothing to miss.

In 1939 I was still too young to really know what war was about. To my schoolmates and myself it was exciting and dangerous, its meaning and significance no deeper than being able to shoot all your friends before your mum called you in for bedtime. But I do recall everyone being very serious around that time. There were long and involved discussions all of which seemed to revolve around Germany and Hitler. The things they were discussing may have been beyond me but the mood that hung over the family was tangible and had a profound effect on me, even at so young an age.

I assume I was at school the day Mr Chamberlain announced that we were at war, as I cannot recall the event with any clarity. There was no television, of course, so the now familiar film of the announcement would not have been seen until the newsreels arrived at local cinemas. What I do recall is that things started to happen at once.

Everything became hustle and bustle. Men of all ages and positions were enlisting in the various forces. My own father tried to join the army but was rejected on the grounds that he had a seriously ill wife to look after. The severity and frequency of my mother's illness had increased dramatically by this time. My uncle George was accepted, however, and in due course disappeared for a time to return in uniform. Much later he would be involved in the evacuation of Dunkirk. The next time we saw him he had serious problems with his leg, clearly as a result of injuries sustained. He never returned to active service, but signed up as an ARP (Air Raid Patrol) warden. I believe my father also served in this capacity. I do know they were both very involved when the air raids began on West Bromwich in 1940.

In the meantime people were sticking brown parcel tape over their windows. This was a precaution to prevent the windows exploding in the event of a bomb blast – the tape would bond the shards of glass together. Tightly fitting black curtains were fitted to all windows and doors to prevent light escaping at night and making the house visible to the bombers. For the duration of the war we would live in this closed in world after dusk in which it was only possible to open a door or look out of a window when all the interior lights had been switched off.

The first time we were actually threatened by the war was when we saw the sky light up over the Coventry side of Birmingham. The bombardment started there, moving on to Birmingham itself, finally reaching as close as West Bromwich around 22 and 23 November 1940. After a while the raids became part of life. The sirens would go off and that terrible deep droning of the German planes would begin, gradually filling the night sky. The heavy ack-ack anti-aircraft guns made as much noise as the bombs as they pursued the droning instruments of death. Metal rained down like confetti and the next morning the streets would be littered with shrapnel. Incendiary bombs started fires all over the place and the noise of fire engines and people shouting and screaming made it feel like the end of the world.

We never once used the shelter, but spent the night in the passageway behind the front door. Whether the shelter would have been safer or not I don't know, but Mother was not fit enough to leave the house for something that basic. On one raid the house to the left of ours took a direct hit. When I went to look at it the next day it had gone down like a pack of cards. Nothing was left but a heap of rubble. Three people – a man, his wife and another lady – were found dead in the cellar, gassed. When the house had collapsed they had been trapped in the cellar with the gas pouring from a fractured main. My uncle George had been one of those involved in the rescue attempt, but in vain, as he explained to us the next morning. It was fortunate for us and the rescuers that the gas didn't ignite. During another raid we lost all the windows at the rear of the house when something exploded in that direction.

With our limited understanding of what was going on, much of what grown ups found terrifying about the war was exciting to lads of my age. It was our favourite game and we spent all the time we had playing bad Germans and good British – even at one stage good Russians. And apart from the fun of collecting shrapnel the morning after a raid, you were also often given time off school as it was considered unsafe to walk through the streets.

Wounded servicemen such as these would convalesce on the hospital balcony and wave to us kids down below. *(Alum Hospital)*

The first time reality hit me was one day when my very close mate Peter from down the road was playing with me. My mother told him it was getting late and he should go home or his mother would be worrying. He left me at about six in the evening. Sadly I was never to see him again.

When I went to call for him the next morning I discovered that Peter, his mother and others, including relations of my aunt, had been blown to pieces and spread across three gardens. They had taken cover in the Anderson shelter in their garden and it had received a direct hit. There was blood everywhere, over everything, making it smell sickly and horrifying. With a hideous irony their house was intact and as far as I could see at the time had not been affected at all.

Another huge bomb fell on the housing area at the bottom of our road killing a lot of people and leaving a crater the size of a small lake. Some things remain in your memory more than others. The paper and confectionery shop was one of the buildings hit by that bomb and I remember that a temporary shop was set up in an existing brick building only yards from the devastation. It continued to be used as a shop for some years after the war and remains to this day on the Birmingham New Road, at the bottom of Hope Street, though it closed long since.

Raids on the town were now becoming more regular and ever more ferocious. Incendiary bombs ignited whole areas and demanded all the vigilance and heroism of the emergency services to keep the fires, buildings and victims under control. Going to school was out of the question. Apart from the ever present dangers, sleeping through the nightly bombardment was impossible. Everyone was exhausted and we would have been incapable of concentrating on schoolwork.

Every evening the family would gather around the wireless to listen to the news, my father plotting the progress of the war on a map of the world which I think came from the *Express* newspaper. He also had an old atlas he referred to when news of events in Britain were reported, but this was rare as anything of possible use to the enemy was heavily classified.

With most able bodied men away at the war, the government asked those too young or too old to join up to form a domestic force to be known as the Local Defence Volunteers (LDV), later the Home Guard. We would see them scaling walls on Beeches Road, armed with poles and wearing tin hats or arm bands in lieu of proper weapons or uniforms, and would think that we children were better equipped to repel an invasion than they were. As time went by they got their uniforms and rifles; some even had tommy guns and the officer had a pistol in his holster. Then their manoeuvres up and down our road had more meaning and caused us to change our opinion, though by then the likelihood of invasion had waned, and those who had been too young at the start were now called up for regular active service. By 1944 the Home Guard was stood down without ever firing a shot in anger, but they had been there and they had been more than ready to do their bit if needed.

In fact a number of things considered necessary at the beginning of the war proved (thankfully) not to be so in the event. Gas masks were one such thing. It had been assumed that since gas had been so widely used by both sides in the First World War, there was a real threat of the Germans turning it on civilian populations in the Second. This threat did not materialise, although it was used on the battlefield. Nonetheless every citizen was issued with a personal gas mask conforming to one of a number of designs. Babies had something akin to a fish tank, but I was old enough to have a standard model. This came in a box with full instructions of how to deploy it in the event of a gas attack. It had an awful rubber smell that made you feel sick when you wore it. Every schoolday we practised putting it on and at the beginning of the war it was compulsory to carry it with you at all times. As the war progressed, however, and the threat fell away, so this practice dropped out until only service personnel invariably carried their masks.

My mother died in June 1943 and I still believe her death was hastened by being caught up in the strafing of West Bromwich High Street by a lone German raider. She arrived home in terrible disorder and her already precarious health declined rapidly. Many parts of the Black Country suffered

An advertisement for Land Girls during the Second World War. 'Dig for Victory' posters were displayed everywhere.

as a result of enemy action. In my own childish world I was unaware of the scale of the devastation, but I did see the damage to West Bromwich town centre and to the city of Birmingham when we went there at the war's end to celebrate VE Day.

As might be expected in a country at war, there were constant shortages and queuing was a way of life. There wasn't much to go round, but what there was was distributed both efficiently and fairly. The hated but workable coupon system was largely responsible for ensuring equality in this respect. With a daily intake of bread and dripping or a crust and butter (or more likely margarine) and fish and chips, I can't really claim to have missed out on much. On the other hand, to this day there are vegetables I have no taste for because I never encountered them as a child. Sweets and chocolate were practically unheard of, though you were occasionally treated to something in this line that was pretty tasteless compared with what we're used to today. I'm sure this resulted from their being made from what little was available. Things I never saw throughout the war included bananas and ice cream. There was a lady near where we lived who made some kind of frozen lollies out of what appeared to be a tasteless and rather watery variety of custard.

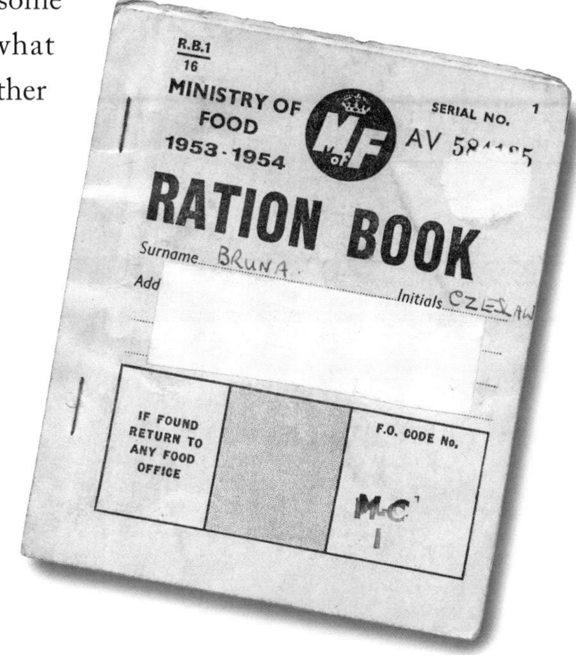

Everyone was required to have a ration book from the start of the war right through to the 1950s. It was cumbersome and bureaucratic in operation but at least it made the situation and the distribution of necessities fair. We got to the point where we didn't know the difference. It seemed as if we had always been on rations.

My father would go from pub to pub in search of beer – 'tenpenny beer' they used to call it then. If a pub could be found that had received a delivery the word would get out and very soon the house would be 'drunk dry'. This seemed to be a routine occurrence. Sometimes we kids would follow our dads from pub to pub, playing outside while they drained the contents. Then, when the landlord put the towel on the pumps, the men would troop off again to the next one reported to have received a delivery. It became like a march of men and kids descending on one ale-house after another. More often than not, the information about the delivery proved to be false, so the march might take in four or more premises for the sake of perhaps only two pints of weak tenpenny beer.

Such was my wartime youth in the Black Country. Like all wars, the hardship, the loss, even the community spirit fades with time. Other things come to demand our attention and if it were not for books such as this or yesterday's heroes parading their medals on designated memorial occasions, it would dwindle from our consciousness. But it is right that we make ourselves aware of the frightful nature of war and the sacrifices of those involved. Nowadays wars are so commonplace that for those not directly involved they can become no more than yesterday's news – more images flickering on a TV screen.

I say this with conviction having spent two years of my own life in the forgotten war of Korea, and having seen young men give up their lives in vain as a result of the actions of some strutting eastern dictator no different to Hitler and Germany five years earlier: it is in the nature of wars that no one ever wins.

5

Pleasure & Leisure

The only real holiday my family ever had was a camping trip to Rhyl in North Wales. Anything else that counted as a holiday to us was really only a day out. Today people think nothing of travelling to the other end of the earth, but before 1950 that kind of thing was the preserve of a very privileged few.

Grimly, it was probably the Second World War that opened up the possibility, or at least the idea, to the wider public. Military service had taken people to Europe and beyond after generations of insularity, just as displaced persons and refugees had brought some of their differences here. The barriers began to break down and people became aware of countries and cultures beyond their own borders.

Before the war, for most people cheap guest house accommodation was the best they could aspire to. Alternatively, camping and caravanning were popular then as they are today, but facilities were somewhat different. In those days a camping holiday was more like joining the army, with basic equipment and very austere living conditions. These days even a tenting holiday is more like staying in a three star hotel than 'roughing it' in the old definition, or really experiencing the great outdoors.

Back then any kind of break, no matter how basic, was outside the means of a large proportion of the population. In magazines of the time you can find advertisements for such delights as a coach trip to France – a week including

The 'magic table' in the Crooked House at Himley – a popular day-trip destination . . .

. . . although 'crooked' was perhaps an understatement.

meals for £9 return. A week in Skegness could be had for £7 10*s* 0*d*. It all seems so cheap by modern reckoning, but you have to remember that a working man was probably only earning £3 10*s* 0*d* a week, so his own fare alone would consume three weeks' wages. What's more, leave was often unpaid, so there would be no money coming in while he was away.

So the day trip was the answer, and the most popular destinations were those that supplied something for the whole family to enjoy. Dudley Castle was a popular choice with my family. Many's the time we went there together, Mother packing as much as Dad could carry, possibly including a heavy glass bottle of pop for me, which was cheaper than buying it at the castle. We walked as far as the main road and caught the Corporation bus all the way to Dudley – a direct route from there with no changes.

Then as now, Dudley Castle had a lot to offer for a family day out.

The waterway under the castle has been pulling them in for generations and can still be visited as part of the Black Country Living Museum.

Feeding time for the sea-lions was always a hit with the kids at Dudley Zoo.

My family at Dudley Zoo in the 1960s. The zoo was still an attractive place to visit, but has since declined. In the picture are (back row, left to right) Bernard Dunn, Alan Sabin, Ed Biggerstaff and my daughter, Janet Bunce; (front row) Andrea Sabin in the pram, Yvonne Dunn, Margaret Dunn, Marion Bunce, Beatrice Biggerstaff and Barbara Sabin. *(Photo by the author.)*

Kinver and Kinver Edge were also good places to go, but fraught with rather more difficulties. Getting there involved three buses – one to Dudley, a second to Stourbridge and the final one to the destination. Once you were there, it seemed like the ideal holiday resort with sands for the kids to play on, walks for the energetic and the famous sand house, which was then still occupied. People actually lived in the caves, which had a hoarding over the front to serve as their only access door, and a small window as their only source of light. Alas, what Kinver lacked utterly was toilet facilities. This was bad enough for us kids – how the grown-ups managed I have no idea. At the time I didn't really care.

If getting there was an undertaking and staying there somewhat uncomfortable, getting home was something akin to Dunkirk. You might have thought that, since the bus company had been ferrying people there all day, they would have taken this fact into account when laying on buses for their departure. But no; around seven o'clock the revellers began to pack up and converge on the single bus stop. No one had given any thought to running extra buses, or even using double-deckers, which would have cleared the gathering queues twice as quickly. By 8 or 9, with a long queue still waiting to be rescued, the bus inspector would announce, 'That's it. There are no more buses.' How the poor man escaped being lynched I don't know. The crowds would press around him and certainly looked as if they had a mind to string him up if relief didn't arrive soon. Finally a bus would be found to Stourbridge but by this time of night the only connection often finished at Dudley. There were no all-night buses then, so you were faced with walking from Dudley to West Bromwich, a marathon that would have taxed the fittest person, which my mother certainly was not. To add to my father's woes, he had to contend with a young lad who had thoroughly exhausted himself with holiday excitement so needed carrying along with what was left of Mother's supplies.

Looking back, you would have thought that this could only happen once before the lesson was learned. But no; it happened time and time again.

Shakespeare's birthplace, Stratford-on-Avon, was a similarly epic expedition. Once all the preparations were complete, you would first get the bus to the boundary outside the Hawthorns. Outside the football club you changed buses (unless you'd been lucky enough to get on the through bus) for Birmingham's Snow Hill railway station. You would make your way from here down to the Bull Ring, then as now a mecca for street entertainers. There

A great day out had by all – Percy Edey and wife Vi with Beatrice Biggerstaff and Mary Bunce.

There'll be another bus along in a minute – if you're lucky. Holy Austin Rock at Kinver.

The entrance to the Crow's Rock Dwelling.

would also be a market with dozens of barrows selling fruit and vegetables. A covered market existed then. Though it would later be extensively damaged in the blitz, it was later cleaned up and the shell of the building returned to its original use for many years after the war.

It was then necessary to join the long queue outside St Martin's church to wait for the Stratford Blue bus. The wait wasn't as bad as it might have been because there was always so much to see in the Bull Ring, but the journey itself seemed endless, despite the fact that there weren't that many stops between Birmingham and Shirley. The journey then continued through country villages such as Henley in Arden, then little more than a high street with a few shops serving the needs of the mostly farming community. It is somewhat different today.

Then as now Stratford was a tourist paradise, with everything the day tripper could wish for – parks, picnic areas, boating on the Avon. While Father demonstrated his boating prowess, or lack of it, Mother would get time to herself with Stratford's wonderful shops. In my memory the summers were always hot and the evenings long, but just as at Kinver they had to come to an end eventually. And, also as at Kinver, that's when the problems began.

Officially the last bus left Stratford at nine o'clock, but there were never enough buses by this time to accommodate all of the town's day visitors, so the same routine was repeated every time. The inspector would tell everyone, 'Sorry, ladies and gentlemen, the last bus has now gone.' The remaining passengers who knew they would not be left stranded became irate and began to threaten the inspector. Then, at the eleventh hour, more buses would arrive and clear the queue.

Snow Hill station, pre-1939. This was the Great Western Railway station and the one my mother and I would use when going to Hornchurch for our sojourns in the Essex countryside (changing at Paddington, of course). On other occasions we used the old New Street station and travelled by LMS (London, Midland and Scottish). Both old stations and railway companies are now no more.

Birmingham's Bull Ring following the bombing in the Second World War. The market is still standing but is only a shell. The double-decker is parked at the stop where we used to catch the Stratford Blue to Stratford-on-Avon.

It cannot be that my family was alone in being always in such dire trouble on these days out. Nobody talked about stress in those days, but these holidays appear to have caused more than they cured. No matter where we went, the need for transport would create some sort of major difficulty. Whether my father always left these things too late and we suffered the consequences I don't know. I do know we weren't the only people doing so. But it did seem that my family always found it a problem.

Our visits to Essex for Mother's health had at least given me the opportunity to see the sea when I was young, although I was sad never to have shared it with my father, who had always to continue working while we were away. Many children around me never saw the sea until they were adults and I often feel the limits on travel that forced you to make your own entertainment in local parks or down by the canal made little day trips or other outings all the more special and memorable, and worth some extra effort.

Many was the time I walked with other boys all the way to Hampstead colliery, the other side of Handsworth, to swim in the nearby canal. Swimming there cost us nothing – a vital consideration – and the water was much cleaner than it was around our way, so the chances of catching some dreadful disease were reduced.

Many families broke their normal routine by taking a paid 'holiday' hop-picking.

An ox-roast at the funfair when it came to the top end of Newton Road, Great Barr, in the 1920s.

George Formby, then Britain's most popular and highly paid entertainer, makes a flying visit to the Black Country in the 1940s on his Norton, with his wife and manager Beryl riding pillion, to promote his latest film.

When I think back on those times, although inevitably I feel a flood of nostalgia, I have to ask myself, were they good days? Not always, but people did make the best of what little they had, and used it to make their lives more acceptable; less of a drudge. Undoubtedly in moments they dreamed of a better life, but they concentrated on enjoying the one they had. No matter how bad things were this was more like living than spending your life hoping to win the lottery, as many now do who never really want for anything. In the '30s people weren't interested in what might be; they didn't squander money on or rack up credit for some future dream. Life was lived one day at a time. Our enjoyment and pleasures may seem small, but they taught us the value of things and gave us a sense of perspective that is little in evidence today.

6

Childhood Memories

Like most kids in my time I don't remember being given much in the way of new toys, except of the home-made variety. What I didn't have in fact I made up for in my imagination – the early development of which serves me well to this day. Mustard tins made excellent buses or lorries. A tin can could also make a perfectly acceptable football and some chalk marks on a back wall a cricket pitch.

I can tell from looking at old photographs that my mother did her best to 'turn me out' each morning looking clean and tidy. How long I stayed that way was another matter. Boyish pursuits such as tree climbing took their toll on clothes and they were often in need of repair. Those were days long before the obsession with designer labels. We didn't worry if patches didn't quite match the colour or texture of the original.

My comics came from the market so were always some weeks out of date, but that didn't matter if you didn't want to follow a serial. The *Beano* and *Dandy* were very much the most popular in those days. We also had *Radio Fun* and *The Magnet*, but the *Dandy* was my favourite with Keyhole Kate and Desperate Dan, with his mammoth cow pies, Happy Days, Chimps' Circus and of course the Disney characters, Mickey Mouse, Donald Duck and Pluto.

It is quite surprising with hindsight how many comics there were back then – *Comic Cuts*, *The Rainbow* and *Mrs Bruin Bear* and the ever-popular *Billy Bunter*, long before he became a TV character.

BUMPER XMAS NUMBER
ALL YOUR COMIC PALS ARE HERE — TO FILL YOU FULL OF XMAS CHEER!
No. 334—DEC. 21st, 1946.
THE DANDY COMIC
2D
KORKY THE CAT
YOUR DANDY CHUMS ALL RAISE A CHEER — THEY'RE MERRY, BRIGHT AND HEARTY, BECAUSE THERE'S DUFF AND GINGER BEER AT KORKY'S CHRISTMAS PARTY.
New
No 5 3d
WAR
NO 15
DESPERATE DAN
"The Daily Mail," Saturday, December 22, 1934—No. 12,063
Christmas to all our Readers
BOYS AND GIRLS
Your Own Picture Paper
THE BEANO COMIC
2D.

As mentioned before, Saturday morning pictures were a must. Timeless features from Laurel and Hardy and a string of films in which George Formby got everything wrong until the last reel, when everything would finally come right and George would even get the girl! They seem very dated and trivial sometimes now when they are rerun on television, but we loved the cowboy films as kids. Gene Autry, Ken Maynard and, best of all, Jesse James, who made us all feel tall in the saddle in the version with Henry Fonda and Tyrone Power that came out in

Gone now but still retaining a place in the hearts of people the world over, Stan Laurel and Oliver Hardy entertained generations of kids, at the Saturday morning pictures, at school film shows and on television. In the lovely market town of Ulverston in Cumbria is a museum dedicated to the duo, founded by the late Bill Cubin and now run by his daughter Marion.

'Hello playmates!' Arthur Askey.

around 1938, and is still rated as one of the best westerns ever nearly seventy years on. Going to the cinema was cheap in those days and gave you a glimpse of another brighter, more exciting world, no matter how brief.

I loved Ted Ray and Arthur Askey on the radio, as well as the 'over the garden wall' routine of Norman Evans. Enoch and Ramsbottom was another hit, with Cecil Frederick and Robbie Vincent. Like most entertainment through the ages, it was the right material for the time – daft, amusing and uplifting. We asked for nothing more.

More adult or sinister material was off limits to us youngsters. Sometimes you might persuade your dad to take you to a horror film, or you could wait outside the cinema and try and persuade a stranger to get you in. You would

A selection of entertainers who were firm favourites with us, including Charlie Chester who went on presenting radio programmes for years after his stand up days were over. Morecambe and Wise only came to national prominence when they were 'discovered' by Lew Grade's ATV in the '60s, but they had been together since 1942 and I remember seeing them in the theatre.

You lucky people – cheerful Charlie Chester.

then join up with your mates who had used a similar ruse. We managed to see some of the gothic goings on of the likes of Boris Karloff and Bela Lugosi, but we really liked Lon Chaney as the werewolf or Frankenstein.

We became amateur film buffs and could identify films by their makers. 20th Century Fox specialised in gangster movies, MGM (Metro-Goldwyn-Mayer) in musicals, and so on. Warner Brothers made both western and gangster films, which tended to be very stylish and serious. I recall seeing the first 'talkie', Al Jolson in *The Jazz Singer*, though I much preferred *The Jolson Story* made years later with Larry Parkes in the starring role.

7

The Death of my Mother

The sixty and more years that have passed since the death of my mother have done nothing to cloud my memory of the event. She died on 3 June 1943 at a mere 35 years of age (she was born on 28 August 1908) and was buried in the family plot (7974W) at West Bromwich cemetery.

In the early morning of that day, while I was still in bed, I began to hear voices in the room below my bedroom, the subdued voices of a number of people, mixed with crying and deep sobbing noises. As a 10-year-old boy I had no idea what was happening or why. I just felt frightened and pulled the bedclothes over me as some kind of protective shield.

Footsteps sounded on the uncarpeted stairs and my bedroom door opened very slowly as if someone who didn't want to disturb me was checking to see if I was awake. As the door opened wider the face of my aunt appeared, tearful and distraught, the locks of her red hair hanging across her face. The poor woman was in a state of shock as she held her hands out to me. The scene is still so vivid in my memory, like a photograph in my mind that has never gone away. She held me tightly in her arms and spoke to me through her sobs, but I couldn't make out what she was saying. Gradually her sobbing subsided and I found myself listening to something about my mother leaving and going to heaven.

I had seen so many people killed in the war that I had a very realistic and un-childlike understanding of what death meant. I was well aware, even at that tender age, that people who died would not be seen again.

I knew my mother had gone into the hospital, and she had never been a well lady, but these facts in no way prepared me for the idea of her dying. Now I can appreciate how awful it must have been for my aunt to have to impart this news to a young child. At the time I pushed her out of the way and ran down the stairs. There seemed to be people everywhere trying to speak to me. I ignored them. I was looking for my father, but the one person who mattered wasn't there. Even now I have no idea where he was. The house was full of people, my mother was dead. Perhaps he was there somewhere but was in no state to see me. Maybe they were protecting him. Maybe they thought they were protecting me.

Such things took a different form in those days – nowadays children have everything discussed with them and everyone seeks 'closure'. I was not even allowed to attend her funeral, just sent to school as if it was a normal day. The first I knew about it, it had already taken place.

I had long been aware that there was something wrong with my mother. She had had frequent bouts of illness and her health was the reason for our visits to my aunt and uncle's place at Upminster Bridge in Essex. At one stage it was considered so imperative that she benefit from the country air that I was sent to school in Upminster. I didn't know as a child what it was she suffered from and only found out many years later that it was a rheumatic heart condition – essentially a weakness in the heart that prevented it from functioning as it should.

It didn't register with me right away, but the moment of my mother's death signalled a change in my life in ways and directions I had given no thought to. I was too young to realise it at the time, but looking back I realise my life was set on a new course by this tragic event and nothing would ever be the same as it might have been had she lived.

My father, George Bunce, and she had married on 18 July 1931 in the register office at West Bromwich. On the marriage certificate my father's occupation was listed as 'brass dresser' and my mother's as 'motor parts assembler'. I later discovered this referred to a job with Joseph Lucas, foremost electrical supplier to the automotive industry. After their marriage they moved in with her parents at 96 Union Street, West Bromwich. I also discovered later that, despite her family all being local, she had in fact been born at Melton Mowbray in Leicestershire at a time when the lack of work in the Black Country had forced her parents to seek employment elsewhere. They had returned to West Bromwich in the early '20s.

Mother's death was also notice that we were again on the move.

I recall her passing with great sadness, but am surprised and grateful that I have so many memories from her short life, and in my mental images she will always be a young woman of 34.

❧ ❧ ❧ ❧ ❧

BIRMINGHAM CO-OPERATIVE
SOCIETY LIMITED
Registered Office: 30-36 HIGH STREET, BIRMINGHAM 4

Member's Share Pass Book

Quote this Code Letter and Number **B** when making Purchases from other Societies.

No. 368842

Name

SPECIAL NOTICE.—Members when making withdrawals are requested to make personal application, but if unable to attend personally, must send a note bearing such member's signature, authorising the person sent to receive the amount, otherwise no money will be paid out.

PASS BOOK OR PURCHASES VOUCHER MUST BE PRODUCED FOR ALL WITHDRAWALS.

Co-operative Printing Society Ltd., Manchester 4.

A vital part of life for many years, the Co-op book. The majority of the English population were members of the Society whose 'divvy' (dividends) could pay for your funeral and little extras for Christmas.

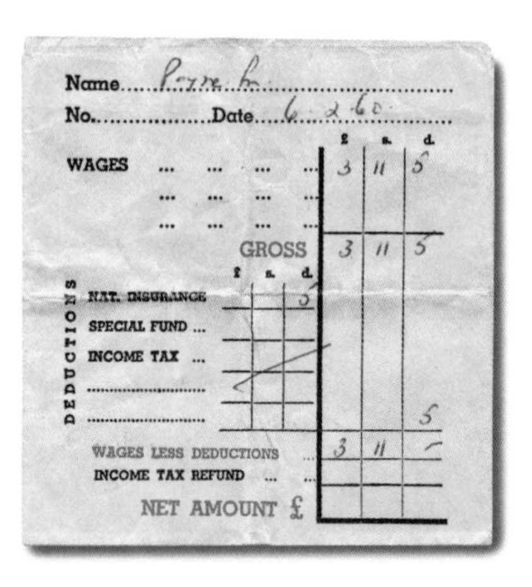

Name ....

No. .... Date 6.2.60

	£	s.	d.
WAGES	3	11	5
GROSS	3	11	5
DEDUCTIONS: NAT. INSURANCE			
SPECIAL FUND			
INCOME TAX			
WAGES LESS DEDUCTIONS	3	11	
INCOME TAX REFUND			
NET AMOUNT £			

A boy's wage packet from 1960 – £3 11*s* 5*d*. A mere twenty years earlier, in the 1940s, a man would have been expected to keep a family on that much. The inflationary spiral was already well underway.

As a little light relief from these tragic events, here are some lines that capture much of the accent and the spirit of the Black Country.

A friend of mine for many years, Ronald Moor is a true gentleman of West Bromwich, an avid supporter of the town's football team, and a poet. Most of Ron's poems are written in the Queen's English, but I hope this one will be both understandable and a means of conveying the rhythm of the place.

He used to work for a company called Peerless Press Ltd, a small printer in the town, and it is a works outing from that worthy establishment to see the Ffestiniog Railway at Porthmadog in Wales that he is describing below:

Our Werks Trip

Our werks trip wert arf grert.
We went dern a mine to look at some slert.
The bloke on the trern said, "Yo cor go dern yet;
Wait till it rerns, then yo'll all get wet!"
It was just like the ghost trern yo get at the fair –
Werter splashed on yer ferce and ruined yer hair.
I bought a slert present – it dae last very long,
For written in Welsh were 'Made in Hong Kong'.
Wax dummies like werkers wus dern there on show,
Unless they wus werkers on a go slow!
The next part of the trip was in wooded cages.
There wern't proper railways, just narrer gauges.
We got to Port Mad Dog and sed were's the sea?
But they all spoke queer, not in English like me.
I hope the next works trip doe goo quite so far –
Why not Tipton and Oldbury via Great Barr?
(Or a visit to Crossroads, but that's gooing too far.)
It doe matter how yo say it, on perper or slert,
Thank you, boss, our werks trip were just grert!

8

The Decline of the Black Country and its Industry

The pace of change has accelerated so much since the end of the Second World War that it is hard to grasp how slow it was in the decades, even centuries leading up to it. Even then the slums and back-to-back houses would remain in existence for another twenty years. Although many of the photographs included here date from a time much earlier than my childhood, the places they depict are very much as I knew them.

Today the big IKEA store just off junction 9 of the M6 draws thousands of customers a year to this little corner of Wednesbury. Few if any of them are aware that this was the site of one of the Black Country's major steel works. F.H. Lloyd's works dominated the landscape half a century ago and employed hundreds of workers. As recently as 1955 the firm was in full expansion, extending its premises and inviting young people to join them for a career in an industry with an assured future. Now it is all gone; the industry itself, the livelihoods of those who chose it as a career, the factories, the services – but it goes wider than that. The demise of such an enterprise also saw the end of its social and support aspects – the works club, the dances, the fishing club, the children's Christmas parties. And Lloyd's was just one of many heavy industrial firms to go from thriving concerns to derelict scars on the landscape in less than a generation. The nation depended on them for the creation of its wealth, but shifts in political viewpoint and the lure of cheaper labour and raw materials elsewhere made them redundant.

Poynton Fruiterers at number 33 Dudley Street, Carter's Green, West Bromwich in around 1926. Mrs Ampliss Poynton poses in her white overall.

Fred Lyndon in his fruiterer's van, 1930s.

Customers and staff outside the Samson and Lion at Harvilles Hill, Hawthorn, Hill Top, in 1927. The pub was probably on the corner of Peter's Street.

Builders and navvies line up for the camera during construction of the Tantany Estate at Hill Top.

Markets were held throughout the Black Country as elsewhere in the realm. Here is the one at Dudley in the 1960s . . .

. . . and this is Walsall market some years earlier.

Alf Loyd stands in the doorway of his shop in Hawekes Lane, Hill Top. Offering a range of provisions including hay, straw, pig feed and 'horse corn', this was the forerunner of the modern supermarket. Poynston's fruit shop was next door to the left of this picture.

This appears to be a church outing from around 1900. Ironic that the trippers were photographed beside an advertisement for Whitbread beer!

Charabanc outing from Carter's Green in 1920. The young girl to the left of the rear wheel is Freda Poynton. Her mother, Ampliss, is next to her and the man with them is probably Mr Poynton.

The sign reads: 'Fountain Inn, feeding strikers' children, July 3rd 1913'. The photograph was taken at the rear of the pub in Wednesbury nearly two months into a strike at the factory of John Russell & Co. The 200 workers from the patent tube works had downed tools on 9 May in support of their demand for improved wages. The owners responded by closing down the works and the strikers suffered severe hardship for many months. The situation was further

exacerbated by the vicar at Old Church, who said the eighteen shillings a week they were being paid was more than enough to live on. His comments caused a great deal of anger and it was deemed necessary to provide a police escort to get him to and from his church. By the time the strike ended in 1913, 37,000 other Black Country workers had come out in support of their cause.

Mary Bunce behind a recreated 1930s shop counter selling many varieties of goods long forgotten but once common in the Black Country.

Right: Neill Humphries is a prime example of the value of an apprenticeship with a company such as Lloyd's. Here he is as a young man gaining the practical experience that enabled him to become a qualified electrician, plumber and builder.

Below: Stepping out at Lloyd's Apprentices' dance party on Friday 25 February 1955. I wonder how many found a partner for life.

9

Final Days in West Bromwich

The death of my mother hit my father very hard. He was lost and bewildered and behaved in very uncharacteristic ways. I was aware that he was going to pieces and I was very concerned, though he wouldn't let me get close to him.

Then, out of the blue, he announced that we were moving again; this time to Handsworth in Birmingham. As the crow flies this was barely five miles down the road, but to me it might as well have been a lifetime away. I sensed that I would be leaving West Bromwich for good and, despite its dirt and grime, it had been my home – a place I felt safe in and was not keen to move from. I made sure my father knew this, but I was too young to have any real say in the matter, so we were soon off to reside with his brother and family in Niniver Road, Handsworth. Of course, for me it meant new schools and the business of making new friends and, little did I know then, not for the last time. My father's wanderings had only just begun and the disruption would go on for years.

At least we had come up in the world from the handcart for this move. A small van removed our last traces from West Bromwich and we began our new life, a life in which father would remarry, move us again and present me with a new brother. It could have gone otherwise, but I'm happy to say that this last was probably the best thing that happened in my life, and I have regarded my brother as my own real kith and kin throughout our lives.

As my schooldays drew to a close and it became time to contemplate earning a living, my father hatched grandiose plans for my future, enrolling me in an apprenticeship at the Grand Hotel in Birmingham with a view to my becoming the manager of some London hotel. That's a story in itself, but it's enough to say here that it wasn't to be. I received my call up papers for the army and spent most of my National Service fighting in the Korean War (1950–3).

When I came out I couldn't settle back into the hotel business. Instead I signed on at Joseph Lucas as a trainee. From nothing, thanks to some of the best training and education available, I rose through the ranks to become executive manager of one of the company's prime sites, but years of seventeen-hour days and responsibility for 1,500 personnel eventually took their toll on me and I retired on grounds of ill health.

I thought that was the end of the story but, after a few years' restful retirement, I was head-hunted by Sheffield company, James Neill, and asked if I would run the Spear & Jackson Garden Tool Company site in Wednesbury as their director of operations on the Neill board. (James Neill was the owner of Spear & Jackson.)

And so after fifty years I was to find myself returning home to a company which had been based no more than two streets away from where I lived as a little boy.

I can't look back on my progress from a lad with patches on his trousers, living in the most humble of abodes, to a valued executive with a comfortable and fulfilling lifestyle without a sense of satisfaction and achievement. My beginnings must have given me something, even if it was only a powerful determination to survive.

Either way, I have never forgotten my roots. Despite many years away the accent has never left me. The dies of Britain's industrial future were cast amid the smoke and soot of these midland towns. And, like molten metal, their crucibles also forged and shaped the people who lived and worked in their pall. I am proud to number myself among them, and to be able to say I was 'manufactured in the Black Country'.

Looking back now to 1944. A good deal had happened to me since my mother had died. I had gone through a period of wildness that I now find hard to explain or justify, but perhaps it was the only way a young boy could express his feelings back then and make people take note.

If I had been a little older, maybe I could have read the signs. As it was I had no inkling that my life was about to change beyond recognition. People were asking me who my father was seeing; did I know the person? Of course, I knew nothing. Why were they asking? What could it mean? I asked my father, but he said forget it, ignore them, tell them to mind their own business, so I was none the wiser.

Suddenly, sometime around June of that year, my father told me to put on my best clothes, comb my hair and so forth because we were going to see a lady at a shop. If you say so, Dad. I remember we went to Hockley Brook by bus from Handsworth and then proceeded on foot along Farm Street, passing on the way a large factory which I was later to know as Joseph Lucas Ltd. I was not to know at that time the part that this company would play in my life, that chapter being still the best part of a decade in the future.

We arrived at the junction with Wheeler Street and my father made for a shop a little way along the road. As I drew up with him I regarded the premises with a slightly quizzical expression. The place had been a fish and chip shop, but not recently. The equipment inside was hung with cobwebs and dust and the windowpanes had the pattern of whitewash that indicated the place was no longer in use. But my father was impatient to move on. He had hesitated by the shop because here was the turning to the yard that was his real destination. I followed him through the puddle strewn entry into the open yard with its twelve houses, two brewhouses and two outside loos. I didn't take all this in on the first visit, of course, because I was too nervous of where my father was taking me and why.

We turned at last into a small gated court, past a loo and a small extended kitchen. I discovered later this had been constructed to wash and peel the potatoes for the erstwhile chip shop. My father didn't need to knock on the door as a lady had stepped out to greet us and was now making us welcome.

The lady was a Mrs Sabin who, as yet unbeknown to me, would be my future stepmother. She was doing her best. She asked me if I liked sweets – clearly from this distance the softening up part of the 'get to know you' process. I think pop was also mentioned. I'm also fairly sure I accepted it. What I can clearly remember is the rather strained atmosphere as my father endeavoured to convince me of the lady's good points and how much I would enjoy living in her house. In his understandable enthusiasm he was caught up in the doomed enterprise of persuading me to accept the lady on our first meeting. With hindsight I'm sure she tried to meet me more than halfway, but it would be many years before our relationship was that of mother and son. Those years would be hell for us both.

The extension to the house in Wheeler Street housed a small kitchen with a coal burner or tub, which was used for boiling the water for bath night (usually Friday). The bath itself was one of

My stepmother Marian with Father.

those free-standing zinc-plated tin affairs. The kitchen led through into a small inner room that served a multitude of purposes – dining-room, sitting-room, even music room – Mrs Sabin was a very accomplished pianist. Such little space as there was to begin with was reduced to near zero by the presence of two wooden easy chairs, a further four upright chairs, a folding table, a glass cabinet and, of course, the piano. Since this room also served as the drawing-room, it was no easy matter finding room for visitors when they came.

On this occasion we didn't share the little room for very long. My father and Mrs Sabin moved into the kitchen and spoke in subdued tones. I assumed their discussions were not for my ears and was still unaware when my father and I took our leave that the house in Wheeler Street was going to be my home for the foreseeable future.

I had no idea that my father had remarried. I later discovered the wedding had taken place in 1944, probably while I was at school. The first I knew of it at the time was one day when he again told me to dress in my Sunday best (not that there was much difference between that and my normal attire). Once more he led me to the house of the lady who lived behind the shop. This time she was not waiting outside to greet us. My dad let himself in with his own key.

He motioned me in and we found the lady standing in the little room looking somewhat nervous. She looked from father to me and back again and my father suddenly announced: 'Meet your new mother.'

Marian Sabin (née Clarke) had been widowed some time before. Unbeknown to me at that time she already had a son called Alan living in an orphanage. It was a very strange way of gaining an instant family, but what could a small boy do about it? I was still young – not yet 12 – and able to adapt to the new direction, so I settled in. In time I also met my new brother who, I'm pleased to say, became closer to me than any blood relation could have been.

10

Welcome to the Grand Hotel

The remainder of my schooling was to take place at Gower Street Boys', close to the Lozells Road and Five Ways at Aston. The building was quite new then having been built in the '30s. Although it wasn't a grand school, it was a good one. The masters were mainly older people as the young folk were still away at the war. Education was of the no-frills variety with a concentration on the three Rs, but the strongest impression of the place was left on me by its corporal punishment.

I cannot recall any period at the school in which we went a full week without several lashes of the cane. It became so commonplace that the headmaster, Mr Mates, and I were practically on first name terms – well, 'Sir' and 'Bunce' anyway. I didn't really want to be familiar. At least he would talk to me while beating my behind half to death with three or six lashes of the headmasterly cane. Sometimes I had already received two or three from the form teacher, Mr Hughes, before being sent on to Mr Mates, so my hands and backside were often red raw.

I soon learned there was no future in going home and complaining. Father's response was to say that I had probably deserved it and if I didn't stop he'd give me another dose.

Such treatment would cause a wholesale war nowadays, but caning and other forms of corporal punishment were the norm in the '30s, '40s and '50s, even the 'enlightened' '60s. A good thing or bad? I cannot really say. I did learn right from wrong, respect and perhaps discipline. Anyway, after seventy years the wounds have healed.

Gower Street had something of a reputation for sorting out boys like me. Their method could be painful but I'm sure Mr Mates had serious doubts that I would ever amount to anything, thinking I would more likely end up as some kind of juvenile delinquent. He made contact some years later and enquired after my well-being. When he found I was succeeding in life he refrained from enquiring again.

I don't make excuses for my rebellious behaviour at school, but I do feel my nomadic existence at that time contributed to it.

I was around 14 when I left school. During my last terms there I had shown that I had some artistic talent and it had been arranged for me to attend a school in Hockley, the Birmingham jewellery quarter, for two days a week. It was wonderful to be in my own little world, doing my own things with little interference from the master, and it gave me great pride to have several pieces of my finished work in silver accepted for exhibition in the Birmingham art section. It clearly demonstrated a bent for working in an engineering environment. But it cut no ice with my father who had already made up his mind in which direction my future was heading.

It was clear he was trying to live his life through me and that meant taking up a career in the hotel trade until I was old enough to become a ship's steward. It worked all right for Deputy Prime Minister Prescott, I suppose. At that time you couldn't enter the school for a career at sea until you were 16, hence the plan to have me apprenticed to the Grand Hotel in Birmingham.

I was just 14 when I was taken to see a Mr Edge, the assistant hotel manager of the hotel in Colmore Row. My father spoke at length with him about his hopes for my success in the trade and so forth. Father clearly saw me as a future manager, but I don't think Mr Edge shared his vision. 'He will start

The Grand Hotel, Colmore Row, Birmingham, was listed as a building of special architectural importance.

Monday at eight o'clock sharp. Have him report to Mr Benson, the restaurant manager in the Colmore Suite. He will have to supply all his own attire, but we do provide, free, two white jackets and an apron each week. The rest – dress shirts, trousers, collars, pattern shoes, etc., is his responsibility. His wages will be nineteen shillings and eleven pence per week.'

The amazing thing about my entire interview was that, apart from the initial introduction, I had neither been asked a direct question, or been given leave to answer one, the whole proceeding having been undertaken between Mr Edge and my father.

At eight sharp on the Monday morning, I would become acquainted with the aforementioned Mr Benson.

11

Through Swing Doors

'Wait there,' said Mr Benson stonily, pointing to a spot by his desk, and turning an altogether more benign countenance on a customer just then leaving the breakfast room, bowed obsequiously, no doubt contemplating a reward for his trouble.

Standing to attention, holding my bag of bits and pieces, I felt out of place and frightened. As I continued to stand there, from time to time other boys dressed in white would come and look at me with 'you'll be sorry' expressions on their faces.

After what seemed like a lifetime, Mr Benson summoned one of the boys: 'Take him down to the locker room and tell him what he has to do. You're responsible for him for the next two days.' The boy indicated that I should follow him and led me first to what was known as the still room. Here countless women were passing trays of tea and coffee to an army of waiters. On the trays also were toast and butter and various expensive looking preserves. We next passed the serving kitchen with its huge hot plate covered with trays of bacon, sausages and other delights, all fed by a dumb waiter from the main kitchen. Lined up behind the hotplate were a row of men in white, with tall chef's hats. The noise was terrific; people shouting instructions and giving out pieces of paper to a clerk at the end of the serving counter. Other boys in white were rushing here and there, being cursed by the older men. Occasionally a girl would appear, but would be treated no better.

The staff at Château Impney at a buffet, *c.* 1940–50. That's me fourth from left.

After a brief tour of the various departments and having been invited to share the locker of the boy who had shown me around, the only smile of welcome in what I perceived to be a tormentor's hell was from a Mr Allen, the man in charge of the locker room.

Once settled in, I was returned to Mr Benson for inspection. 'Put your hands out. No, you stupid boy, turn them over. I want to see your nails. They are disgraceful. Go and scrub them,' he barked. Then turning a suddenly smiling face to a customer, 'He's new.' He pointed at me. 'Very new, but we will lick him into shape – if it is at all possible.' Mr Benson was the restaurant manager and bore a strong resemblance to Reg Holdsworth (Ken Morley) in Coronation Street.

To me the Grand Hotel seemed like something prehistoric, peopled by customers who were still regarded as gods, long after the empire had died. I was to work a long day, eleven hours at a shift with a break in the afternoon from three to six. I vowed I would never set foot in the place again, but Father had different ideas, so I duly presented myself at eight the next morning.

Dressed to kill. Me in my tails at the Grand in 1950.

'What time do you call this?' demanded Mr Benson, the self-appointed overlord of Great Britain.

'Eight o'clock, sir,' I replied.

'Yes, I know it's eight o'clock,' he blustered, 'but you are supposed to be here in time to prepare everything for inspection, so you are ready to start at eight o'clock.' I remember standing there, puzzling over this man, my loathing for him all-consuming. He was clearly out to break any sign of spirit in me and force me to succumb to the discipline of his silly empire.

Looking back on it now, I realise that this was the start of my preparation for the real world. He was never able to break my spirit, as much as he tried. And he wasn't alone. In later life the army tried even harder and failed. But what Mr Benson did teach me was discipline, presentation, cleanliness, a sense of purpose, an eye for detail – along, of course, with all the skills required to be proficient in the worlds of service and catering.

The Grand was a large hotel with many different dining-rooms, but my duties were confined to the breakfast room in the morning, the Grosvenor Room at lunchtime and the French Restaurant in the evening. A new boy such as myself was seconded to a higher rated individual whose training scheme seemed to involve getting you to fetch and carry, lay tables and so forth, In other words, for at least a year you were a dogsbody or skivvy. At the end of breakfast all tables would be moved to the side of the room and some of us would be detailed to sweep the carpet, with brushes or vacuum cleaners. Others would fill the cruets, clean the silver and wash and prepare the glasses for the next day; all this for a pittance!

Cleaning the dining-room was thought of as a task you could do in your own time. Likewise after lunch you would be expected to wash and dry hundreds of glasses before being allowed to depart from the area. It was hard work and the employers exploited you to the limit. In the better hotels everything was in French, and you were expected to learn quickly and acquire an understanding of the language or life would be most difficult. Without it you would not be able to convey your order to the kitchen, or to know when it was ready! I can still hear the cries of 'Cassoulette d'escargots au Roquefort or fruite tour d'argent,' being shouted by the chefs and waiters of the day. Wines were another speciality you had to master. You needed to be sufficiently knowledgeable to recommend a choice of wine – Bourgogne, Côtes du Rhône – and know from which district they originated.

At the end of two years at the Grand I decided to apply for the position of *demi-chef* at the Grosvenor Hotel in London. I'd come a long way since my first day with Mr Benson and my application and interview were successful, so I was off down to the capital for the next stage in my wanderings.

At first I lodged with a lady and her daughter at Clapham Junction, but I didn't like the area much and soon found better lodgings with a Mrs John not far from the Oval cricket ground. She was a kindly, motherly type, which was just as well, as it turned out my previous landlady had taken a whole month's worth of coupons from my ration book. Mrs John kept me for a month on a share of her rations. I will always remember that dear lady and her kindness to me.

I progressed well at the Grosvenor; so much so that I was given a prominent position, that of number one in the dining-room. This meant better money, but also of course brought greater responsibilities. I was now earning some £8 to £10 per week – not bad at all in those days for a boy of 16 – as well as a percentage of the 'trunk', a pooled tipping system.

Being in London also meant that on my time off I could go and visit my aunt and uncle in Hornchurch, so it was all working out very well. But, alas, the arrangement was not to last very long as my father wanted me back in Birmingham. The management of the Grosvenor did everything they could to change my father's mind, offering a long-term (week's) break with half pay if I would return. But I was still a minor and father was adamant; it was back home for me. He'd even hired a car in which to fetch me. So after only six months in London I found myself at the Midland Hotel, the sister to the Grand. Both hotels were owned by the Gordon family. Although I was unhappy about the move and didn't really settle in, at least I saw more of father, who had also joined the hotel as a *sous-chef*.

The French Restaurant

I can claim to have 'rubbed shoulders' with some notable celebrities during the '50s. Frank Sinatra asked me to join him for a drink at the Queen's Hotel, and later introduced me to his then wife, Ava Gardner who, to say the least, would have made any man's toes curl! There was also Anna Neagle whom I got on with very well during her stay at the Grand, partly by ensuring that her rice pudding was the way she liked it – with the skin on top. I would wait for her after the show and we would enjoy a chat before calling a taxi around one o'clock in the morning. William Hartnell (later to be the first Doctor Who) was another. I admired him for his down to earth attitude. We enjoyed a quiet pint in the snug bar downstairs at the Midland on numerous evenings during his stay. Oh, happy days!

Sadly not all 'celebs' were such nice people. Gilbert Harding was very well known in the '50s from appearances on radio and television 'chat shows' and as a panellist on *What's My Line?* He was staying at the Grand one night, long after the bar had shut, and made it clear in no uncertain terms that he required drinks. He also required certain other things, and made no bones about that either. I put his behaviour down to his being the worse for drink and tracked down the assistant manager for the bar keys.

This had taken a little time, so when I returned to Harding's suite, probably as a result of my indifference to his sexual desires, he started to rant and rave like a madman. I informed the manager, assuming that would be an end of the matter. Instead, he returned telling me that I had insulted Mr Harding and he was demanding my instant dismissal.

I advised him in my turn that I would proceed to the man's suite and separate his head from his body unless he shut his foul mouth and refrained from bothering me again.

I heard no more on the subject. I think I behaved in the correct way in the first instance, so had no regrets about my subsequent comments or actions. Thankfully, not too many of his sort were around and most were able to deal with their fame – which, in most cases had been earned after years of hard work and dedication to their profession.

Ava Gardner *(above)* and Frank Sinatra *(left)*. I was so starstruck on being asked to join them for a drink at the Queens Hotel in Birmingham that I completely forgot to ask them for their autographs – which I have regretted ever since.

Gilbert Harding was quite a celebrity in the 1950s, especially well known for his appearances on BBC TV's *What's My Line?* Eventually he was sacked for calling it 'an idiotic game', an example of a lack of tact and grace that was just as evident in his private life. He had a drink problem and was indiscreet to say the least about his sexual orientation at a time when it was not socially (or legally) acceptable. He already had a reputation as a very rude and self-opinionated individual. Unfortunately I was in the wrong place at the wrong time and was at the receiving end of both his rudeness and his sexual advances.

I was able to socialise with many of the stars of the day and was on first name terms with quite a few of them. It was an exciting period and I was still young enough to be a little vain and to bask in the reflected limelight of the show world. I'm not sure if I would wish to do the same now, but for that period of my life it was a thrill to be able to mix socially with such people. On Saturday nights I would be in attendance at dinner dances, events which led to my appreciation of light music and also provided an opportunity to appreciate the ladies in their evening dresses, swirling around the dance floor.

By now I had moved up the ladder, having responsibility for several dining tables and a staff working for me. If it did nothing else, this did wonders for my confidence in my own abilities. Having been there only a few months, I applied for full *chef de rang* at the Château Impney Hotel in Droitwich,

Anna Neagle, a lovely lady who had a special taste for rice pudding with the skin left on. She treated me well and will always occupy a warm place in my thoughts.

This wonderful photograph captures the beauty and fine setting of Château Impney.

working for Ralph Edwards. This was a very fine, first-class hotel, set in extensive grounds and originally built in the form of a château for a salt millionaire, John Corbett, and his French wife. The clientèle there could be even more upmarket. As well as film stars, it was not unusual to be welcoming royalty to the château.

The job there was highly demanding, as you had to prepare the meals at the table. But, for me, time had moved on. I was now getting on for 18 and National Service loomed. A period in the armed services was compulsory in those days for people found fit for active duty. Service could have been in any of the three services, Navy, Air Force or Army, but most went to the Army, and I was no exception.

Seeing this coming, I decided to move back to the Grand and re-establish my position before call-up. That way the hotel would be required to keep my position open pending my demob. I continued there until 1950 when my papers arrived and I was told to report to Oswestry for initial training and kitting out, prior to be assigned to a regiment for full training.

My days in the hotel business were over for the time being. By this time my earnings had grown considerably. I had learned my trade the hard way, but had become successful and comfortably off, so it was not a welcome discovery that the Army was going to pay me a mere £1 5*s* 0*d* a week. Ten shillings of that would be going to my stepmother, leaving me the princely sum of fifteen bob to live on and support the lifestyle of a gunner in the Royal Artillery. After a few weeks things became even worse when I was accused of losing some of my clothing and a further seven shillings a week was deducted each week to pay for it. Two years into my Army career I was informed that this had been an error and all the money I had paid was reimbursed. It could only happen in this country.

12

It's Too Late Now . . .

It's too late now to be having thoughts of climbing Mount Everest or swimming the Channel. Perhaps the time has past for any ambitions I may have had a lifetime ago. How long it now seems since I started out down the road of life, not even knowing what it meant or where it might lead. Looking back, I had no knowledge of the word or concept of ambition. All I set out to do was survive. It seemed as much as we could hope for in that blighted landscape, in that awful war.

Life is lived in a constant state of change. You gain new friends, lose old ones; your circumstances improve sometimes – other times they worsen – but things are never static. Does it really matter that we miss out on some things along the way? It's not a perfect world and we can't have everything we want. If we did, the game would be over and there would be no point in continuing. It is because they are set against our failures that our successes are so sweet, so worth attaining.

It's too late for regrets, though I wish I had been closer to my father during his short life. I wish I had been able to ask the questions that only crystallised in my mind when it was already too late. I wish I could have sat down with him and explained that, while I may not have fulfilled his ambitions for me, I did live a satisfying life in which I achieved goals of my own. I'm sorry for the hard and unrewarding years he suffered in the 1930s and for his poor health in the years before he died. It all now seems so long ago. I'm sorry I wasn't old enough to appreciate my stepmother, who I'm sure did her best for me in those early years. Wisdom comes with age and often too late to make amends.

What also seems to come with age is membership of the growing army of moaners that maintains that things were better in their day. Better? It's probably always a debatable claim and certainly couldn't be made with any conviction by those growing up in the Black Country in the 1930s. A world war happened in my 'good old days', but practically every generation since can make that statement. Rather than dwell on things that were and what might be waiting for us around the next corner, if I've learned anything it is that we should live, and enjoy, life while we can. You won't get another crack at this life, so make the most of it.

About the Author

Gordon Bunce was born in West Bromwich, Staffordshire, which now forms part of the West Midlands. His early schooling was at various comprehensives before attending Chance Technical College and Hilver College in Birmingham. He later studied consultative management at the Japanese Union of Science and Engineering. He was later to qualify as a Fellow of the British Institute of Management.

Gordon was on the Executive of Joseph Lucas Electrical Co. Ltd, and also on the Board as Director of the Spear & Jackson Tool Company.

Gordon has successfully written several books about Joseph Lucas Co. Ltd and writes articles about antique toys for a well-known national magazine.